CONTESTED CHRISTMAS

Books by C. Dale Brittain, available in print, as ebooks,
and as audio books.

<u>The Royal Wizard of Yurt series</u>
A Bad Spell in Yurt
The Wood Nymph and the Cranky Saint
The Lost Girls and the Kobold [novella]
Mage Quest
Below the Wizards' Tower [novella]
The Witch and the Cathedral
Daughter of Magic
A Long Way 'Til November [novella]
Is This Apocalypse Necessary?
My First Kingdom [omnibus of *Bad Spell, Wood Nymph,* and *Mage Quest*]
Third Time's a Charm [omnibus of the three novellas]

<u>Yurt the Next Generation</u>
The Starlight Raven
An Autumn Haunting

The Sign of the Rose: A Medieval Romance
Ashes of Heaven
Shadow of the Wanderers/Voima
Count Scar [with Robert A. Bouchard]
Heretic Wind [with Robert A. Bouchard]

Positively Medieval: Life and Society in the Middle Ages
Contested Christmas [essay]

CONTESTED CHRISTMAS

C. Dale Brittain

Originally published as an ebook September 2014

First paperback edition October 2018

www.Daimbert.com

ISBN: 172746690X
ISBN-13: 978-1727466904

CONTENTS

1. THE CONTESTED MEANING OF CHRISTMAS

Ah, the "true meaning of Christmas." Between Thanksgiving and New Year's one hears the term constantly, on everything from made-for-TV movies playing essentially non-stop, to exhortations that we all wish each other Merry Christmas rather than Happy Holidays, to websites devoted to tips on crafting handmade ornaments.

But the "true meaning of Christmas" is highly contested. Most would agree that over-commercialization is ruining Christmas, even as great piles of expensive and beautifully wrapped presents, to make children's eyes glow with excited anticipation, are considered part of the season's true meaning.

Magazine articles in November and December routinely urge readers to simplify their holiday celebrations to avoid stress and over-spending, even while other magazines—and often the same ones!—show elaborately decorated interiors, provide recipes for lavish feasts, and contain ads promoting luxury purchases.

Christmas is supposed to require snow, even though in

the US, where the song "White Christmas" is recorded by dozens of artists, the majority celebrate the holiday with no snow on the ground. And in the southern hemisphere, including Australia, Christmas comes in the middle of the summer. (December snow, interestingly, puts one in the Christmas spirit, while January snow makes one yearn for Florida.) Family, faith, and friendship are identified with 4H and with Kwanzaa, yet are also considered true aspects of Christmas.

Part of the true meaning of the Christmas season revolves around its (relative) shortness, extending only from Thanksgiving to New Year's. During a period of not much over a month, it is expected that we will pack in a good six months' worth of shopping, decorating, eating, socializing, worshipping, and attending concerts—not to mention relaxing and taking it all in. Everybody knows about the Twelve Days of Christmas, which traditionally began on Christmas Day and ended on January 6, the Feast of the Wise Men. But in practice the US has forty days or so of Christmas, and the season is definitely over well before Twelfth Night.

(New Year's both recapitulates the gaiety and celebration that are supposed to define Christmas and marks the end of the season. It's easy to tell when Christmas is over. It's when the TV news anchors and sports commentators remove the poinsettias from their desks. This happens on January 2.)

The holiday comes laden with powerful and conflicting expectations, expectations that require a great deal of work, organizing, and spending in order to achieve the simple joys that are supposed to convey its true meaning. The season is intended to be one of mirth and joy, and so we set to work with grim seriousness to make sure that the mirth's meaning is properly joyous. As everyone strives to make this the best (and doubtless truest) Christmas ever, it is worth pondering: why is Christmas the only holiday that gets to have a true meaning?

2. THE TRUE MEANING OF EASTER?

It certainly isn't the religious aspect that makes Christmas special. You never see a heart-warming TV movie about a family discovering the true meaning of Easter. Yet Easter is a much more important Christian holiday than is Christmas. Easter has been celebrated since the earliest church, but Christmas began only as a fourth-century reaction to pagan efforts to make December 25 a birthday for the sun-god Apollo. After all, anyone can have a birthday, but rising from the dead has got to be special.

Incidentally, the winter solstice on December 21, Christmas (and Apollo's birthday) on the 25th, and New Year's are now spread out over a ten day period, but originally they were all celebrations of the darkest day of the year, the solstice, and the beginning of the sun's return as the days start to grow longer. Keeping track of that pesky leap year, celebrated every four years except when it's not, messes calendars right up.

The darkest days of the year were an important time for celebration long before the spread of Christianity. The Romans, the Greeks, the Babylonians, everyone had one or more holidays or feasts around that time, times for food and drink, for merry-making with friends, for gifts, and often for a fairly raucous breakdown of normal social conventions. It is perhaps ironic that many of these ancient pagan aspects are continued in what is supposed to be a thoroughly Christian holiday.

Comparing the celebrations of Christmas and Easter indicates how differently the holidays are viewed. When was the last time you saw a billboard, "Keep Christ in Easter"? Probably never. How many singers bring out an Easter album? Remarkably few. How many radio stations blast the airways with Easter songs non-stop all during Lent? None at all. Compared to big discussions of whether Santa Claus is a jolly old elf, a saint, or a satanic being (in Dijon in 1951, the cathedral priests burned Père Noël in effigy on Christmas Eve as a pagan impostor), the Easter Bunny gets off remarkably easy. For a great many people, Easter means chocolate eggs and new spring outfits, and maybe that annual attendance at church.

Perhaps it is not worth thinking too deeply about rabbits, a symbol of promiscuity in most cultures, laying little brown pellets that children are encouraged to eat. Sex and coprophagia, not a good combination. At least the rabbits do not represent any "true meaning."

Perhaps Easter's meaning is so obvious that it doesn't need to be defended or even identified. "He is risen" is such a powerful message that it speaks for itself, whereas "He is born" needs a number of details filled in. But a celebration of Jesus's birth back in the year 1 (or 4 BC, depending on how you calculate Herod's reign) is only a fraction of Christmas's "true meaning."

Early in American history, Pilgrims and Puritans denied that Christmas actually had any true meaning or religious significance. Pointing out (correctly) that shepherds watch their flocks by night in the spring, during lambing season, not in midwinter, ministers argued that Easter, not Christmas, should get all the attention.

Puritans could even be fined for celebrating Christmas, because back in England a lot of the season's celebration had involved heavy drinking, and they wanted none of that. The Puritan preacher Cotton Mather lashed out at Christmas celebrations, which he said were marked by "mad mirth, by long eating, by hard drinking, by lewd gambling, by rude reveling." But over the next few centuries a veneer (at least) of religiosity established itself around Christmas.

3. A VENEER OF RELIGIOSITY

Heavy metal bands record "O Holy Night." I have heard them.

For a country with an enormous variety of religious faiths and a self-conscious determination to avoid privileging any of them, the US sure looks Christian every December. Theologically informed songs fill the playlists of radio stations that normally play rock-'n'-roll or easy listening. Children may sing the distinctly secular "Jingle Bells" and "Frosty the Snowman" in school, but overtly Christian carols are played from mall to supermarket to car radio.

The "round young virgin" (as many children think of her) comes in for a lot of attention. Doctrinal issues like the immaculate conception of that round virgin are known to pop up. Manger scenes appear in every town and village, sometimes on a church lawn but sometimes in a village park. Christmas is the only federal holiday explicitly based on a religious celebration (having been so since 1865).

It might be said that if secularists are at war with Christmas, then Christmas is winning. If getting people to say Happy Holidays is the best weapon those warring on

Christmas have, then they have thoroughly and long since lost.

Cries to "put Christ back in Christmas" often fixate on the abbreviation "Xmas," with its supposed reduction of Christ to a cipher. In fact, that X is not really an X. It is a *chi*, the Greek letter which begins the word Christ in Greek, the original language of the New Testament. The shorthand abbreviation of X for Christ goes back to medieval monks, who could never be mistaken for secularists.

For that matter, Protestants who worry about a "war on Christmas" never seem to call for putting the Mass back in Christmas.

A further difficulty of defining Christmas purely as religious is how small a detail Jesus's birth is in the Bible. The gospels of Mark and John start with him as an adult. What is usually taken as The Christmas Story, with Mary and Joseph having to go to Bethlehem and finding no room in the inn, then being visited by shepherds (presumably ones watching for lambs), is only in Luke. Luke has no wise men. Matthew has wise men but no shepherds, and this gospel implies that Mary and Joseph had always lived in Bethlehem, rather than coming to town for taxation purposes. Absolutely nothing in the Bible suggests that Jesus's followers celebrated his birth with midwinter festivities.

So religious observance is part of Christmas's "true meaning," but it certainly is not all of it.

4. GENEROSITY

Christmas is a season of generosity, both to one's friends and family and to worthy organizations. Ebenezer Scrooge in "A Christmas Carol" marks his transformation from miserable tightwad to someone who understands Christmas's true meaning by making a generous gift to help the poor. It helps that the holiday falls just a week before the end of the year, so that tax-deductible gifts made at Christmas will reduce that year's tax burden. But shouldn't it seem odd that we are exhorted to "remember the less fortunate among us" at Christmas but not at Easter?

In many a heart-warming broadcast special, a young person decides to forego an expensive gift and discovers the true meaning of Christmas by donating it to a poor family. You don't see him donating his Easter eggs.

Yet gifts to such young people from adults constitute an aspect of the true meaning of Christmas for those adults. Parents who live paycheck to paycheck still feel compelled to spend heavily on presents for their children. Curiously, when the children are small, many American parents deny with some fervor that they bought these presents. Instead of being purchased in a big-box store, gifts are characterized as magically created at the North Pole. Thus, they are (theoretically) stripped of commercialism—although the parents who insist on the reality of Santa's toyshop, not the children themselves, are the only ones who even know what commercialism is.

Even after the children stop believing in Santa, parents feel compelled to wrap their presents. Just to hand a child a new shirt or a book or toy, all agree, totally violates the spirit of Christmas. The present must be wrapped—even if only by being pushed into a gift bag with tissue paper on top—in order to take it out of the realm of something bought in a store and into the magical world of Christmas.

Such gifts can also take on semi-religious overtones: just as the wise men brought gifts to the baby Jesus, so parents should bring their own children gifts—even if not gold, frankincense, and myrrh. That the Feast of the Wise Men is twelve days after Christmas does not diminish the centrality of gifts to Christmas itself.

While in practice, most of the time in human history, the less powerful made offerings to the more powerful, an important part of most mid-winter celebrations has been an inversion, where the powerful made gifts to their subordinates. In the nineteenth century, there was a great deal of nostalgia for a (probably imaginary) past, when tenants—even slaves in the antebellum South—were properly grateful for small gifts from Master. When, especially in the rapidly-growing industrial cities, the deserving poor did not seem to behave as decorously or as deservingly as the well-to-do thought they should, these gifts began to be bestowed instead on children.

Christmas-time generosity, which once meant food and drink and small amounts of money for the wassailers who came from outside the home, is now directed principally at those within the home, even while the organized charities—and newspaper carriers and doorkeepers and hairdressers—keep alive the need to remember others.

In the first part of the twentieth century, Christmas

presents were only for children, not for adults. Even now, in some western countries such as France, the children are the primary gift recipients while the adults find the true meaning of the holiday in oysters and foie gras. Yet these days in the US, gifts to adults, especially expensive electronic gifts, are expected. The retail industry of course encourages this thinking, to the extent that it almost seems one's patriotic duty to spend heavily during the month of December in order to keep the American economy humming.

Those parents who plan ahead may shop for presents year-round, and this is fine, yet everyone agrees that it is Just Wrong for stores to put up Christmas decorations immediately after Halloween, or even sometimes before. An artificial tree decorated with Jingle Bears ringing out Christmas favorites (especially "The Little Drummer Boy") is reviled by shoppers and store clerks alike in October, even though two months later it will be considered entirely appropriate.

Over-emphasis on buying things is routinely said to detract from the true meaning of Christmas, as the Grinch who stole Christmas discovered in the Dr. Seuss classic when he took away all the presents but could not take away the fellowship and joy. Yet the commercialization of Christmas is embraced even while it is deplored. The recent trend to have stores open on Thanksgiving, to get a head start on Christmas shopping, although denounced as distracting from Thanksgiving's true meaning (the only time that particular holiday gets to have a true meaning), means that thousands of people wait in the cold for the doors to open and trample each other in a mad search for bargains.

The gift-giving of the Christmas season has even infected Hanukkah, a fairly minor Jewish holiday that once involved children playing with the dreidel and being given small gifts of money. Now some Christian-Jewish mixed families feel compelled to make the eight nights of Hanukkah into eight nights of presents, and Jewish parents have been known to procure a "Hanukkah bush" that looks remarkably like a Christmas tree. The children presumably welcome this opportunity to receive more gifts, with sparkling eyes and eager anticipation.

5. SANTA CLAUS: THE BACKSTORY

Santa is a central part of the modern American true meaning of Christmas, even though he became so only in the nineteenth century, as exemplified in the poem, "A Visit from Saint Nicholas," or, as it is now better known, "The Night Before Christmas." The centrality of Santa Claus is indicated by the virtual requirement that parents of small children take those children to the mall to sit on Santa's lap, in spite of their understandable fear of a large stranger in a false beard. Preferably they have their pictures taken with him. Most preferably of all, they are not sobbing in terror during the photo shoot.

British-heritage Americans obtained Santa from the Dutch in New York at the beginning of the nineteenth century. Or rather they created Santa out of elements that included Dutch heritage, and from New York he quickly spread to the rest of the US.

Santa is a strangely transmogrified version of Saint Nicholas—Sint Niklaus (or Sinterklaas) as the Dutch know him. As early as the seventeenth century, the saint was believed to reward good Dutch children of prosperous parents with gifts. Even now in the Netherlands, Sint Niklaus comes up the canal in his canal boat on his feast day, December 6, to bring presents to good little boys and girls and to put coal in the wooden shoes of the bad ones.

Enterprising American children have been known to argue that it would be most appropriate to get presents on December 6, Saint Nicholas Day, on the Feast of the Wise Men on January 6, and on most of the days of the month between, including all of Hanukkah, Christmas Eve, Christmas itself, and (why not?) Kwanzaa. This argument has never succeeded.

The American Santa has migrated from Saint Nicholas's feast day on December 6 to the 25th. He has also migrated quite a bit from his original identity as a bishop of Myra in what is now Turkey to someone who lives at the North Pole with Mrs. Claus, the elves, and all those reindeer.

The fourth-century bishop of Myra, who could have been a historical figure, was part of the Byzantine world, centered on the New Rome of Constantinople, the home of what came to be Greek Orthodoxy. Nicholas was considered a saint in subsequent centuries, with a special interest in the well being of children. Most famously, he supposedly brought back to life lost children who had been chopped up and put into the stew pot by an unscrupulous innkeeper. In addition, he anonymously contributed the necessary money for dowries so that the daughters of an impoverished man could marry suitably, rather than being sold into prostitution. (Nicholas is also the patron of sailors, but that's a different story.)

Nicholas has moved around a lot. When Russia became Christian during the ninth and tenth centuries, Nicholas became the special patron of the Russian Orthodox church. He has never brought Christmas presents to good little Russian boys and girls, however. The closest figure to the American Santa there is Father Frost, who, while cloaked in attributes of "traditional" Russia, has no apparent religious aspects. (Indeed, while Soviet Russia was officially atheistic, the government encouraged a "New Year's celebration" with a decorated tree and gifts to the children from Father Frost.)

Meanwhile, back at Myra, a tomb considered to be that of Saint Nicholas was known for oozing oil, identified as myrrh, reputed to have great healing powers. The myrrh and the healing powers continued to accompany him when, after his region of Asia Minor fell under Turkish control in the eleventh century, priests from the southern Italian city of Bari stole his bones and whisked them off to their own city, where they still remain. Several of these bones, however, especially finger-bones, have been taken (doubtless with great piety) to other cities over the centuries, and both the Venetians and the Russians have claimed at various times that they themselves now have the saint's entire body, although those in Bari deny this.

During the Italian Renaissance, Saint Nicholas (San Niccolò) societies were formed, following the saint's legendary example, to provide dowries to poor-but-deserving girls, girls who would have had trouble contracting appropriate marriages if they could not bring dowries to their husbands. Stained glass images of the saint from the period show him dressed in his red bishop's robes, coming down the chimney with a sack full of dowries to drop into the laps of the poor-but-deserving girls, who had fallen into exhausted sleep by the kitchen fire after finishing scrubbing all the pots. The lap was symbolic, because a dowry could keep a girl who otherwise couldn't get married from having to go into the municipal brothel.

This image lurked in the background of those who created the modern image of Santa Claus in the nineteenth and early twentieth century. It is probably not good to dwell on Santa and his gifts as a preserver of chastity anymore than it is good to think too much about the chocolate eggs.

The modern Santa, although having roots in a much older tradition, was a new construction in the nineteenth century, created to personify the home- and child-centered nature of Christmas—as opposed to the drunken revelry version. Back in the sixteenth century, Martin Luther himself had tried to replace the then normal gift-giving of New Year's with a greater focus on Christmas Day. This led to a need for someone to bring children gifts on that day.

But it was not until a good two hundred years later that this gift-bringer began to take definitive shape, Santa Claus in the US, Father Christmas in England, Père Noël in France, the *Weihnachtsmann* in Germany, the Christmas gnome in Sweden, Father Frost in Russia. The name Kris Kringle, sometimes now used as a nickname for Santa, is actually a corruption of *Christkindl,* the Christ child, who also brings gifts in some German-speaking areas. Nicholas, with his patronage of children and a feast day less than three weeks earlier, migrated to Christmas quite easily.

His elves are a much later addition. In Protestant Europe, he was often accompanied instead by a so-called Blackamoor from Spain—the ancestor of the Black Peter who still acts as Saint Nicholas's "helper" in modern Belgium. The original version of the black companion, Struwwelpeter in an influential German poem from the 1840s, suggested a double version, the friendly saint who brings presents and the semi-demonic figure who punishes wicked children. Ironically, in some places Nicholas himself got to be the bad half of the pair, handing out coal and switches as Kris Kringle gave children toys.

While there are thus many antecedents to Santa Claus, the modern version was a deliberate creation, an effort to construct something new which claimed to be old and traditional. Santa is quintessentially American, and all the European Christmas-time gift-givers have been heavily influenced by him.

What might be called the "birth" of Santa Claus took place at the very beginning of the nineteenth century with Washington Irving, now better known for his "Legend of Sleepy Hollow." He portrayed Santa as the personification of all that should be joyous, convivial, and old-fashioned about Christmas, a holiday based on hearty good fellowship, not on material goods or drunken carousing.

"Old Christmas" was a repeated concern for Irving, who described as nearly forgotten such Christmas traditions as mince pie, the Yule log, and Morris dancing, all of which gained new attention through his books (which was of course his intention). In his *Sketch-Book,* he created an imaginary old-fashioned time in England when the kindly landlord of Bracebridge Hall and his sturdy and deferential tenants (grateful for small gifts from Master) still knew how Christmas ought to be celebrated. But a kindly English landlord was not enough.

In his *Knickerbocker's History,* he celebrated New York's Dutch roots, at a time when the recently established United States were feeling less than friendly toward the British (the War of 1812 and all that) and looking for something else to claim as our heritage. The Dutch were already associated with winter festivities because New Yorkers imported Dutch cookies as a New Year's delicacy—cookies often stamped with Saint Nicholas, probably because they had been baked in Holland for December 6 celebrations.

In a burst of creativity almost equal to his invention of the Headless Horseman, Irving came up with Santa Claus (he called him Saint Nicholas but it was obviously Santa), a kindly old Dutchman who, he asserted, represented the good old-fashioned celebration of Christmas and whose ceremonies were observed by all "ancient families of the right breed."

Here for the first time Santa flew through the night on the eve of Saint Nicholas Day, puffing on his pipe, landing his horse and wagon on rooftops. He then slid down the chimney and took gifts out of his breeches' pockets to stuff into good children's stockings. He rose back into the air by "laying his finger beside his nose." Tidbits from a millennium and a half of Saint Nicholas stories either inspired Irving or were added to the basic story. By a decade or two into the nineteenth century, Santa had become a quintessential part of the New York winter celebration, and from there quickly spread to other parts of America.

He soon outcompeted other versions of a gift-bringer, some of whom, like Santa, were based ultimately on Saint Nicholas. In southeastern Pennsylvania, for example, an area with many German immigrants, children expected a holiday visit from Belsnickle (a name derived from a low-German term meaning "Nicholas in furs"). Belsnickle, who bore a strong resemblance to Struwwelpeter, was a frightening fellow, played by someone in blackface and a wig. He would come to the house, demand if the children had been good or bad, and distribute treats to the good ones and snap his whip at the bad ones. In some cases Belsnickle, or even a whole gang of Belsnickles, would demand food and drink from householders rather than distributing gifts to children. The kindly Dutch-inspired Santa Claus, much less terrifying (and much more invisible, coming while children were asleep), soon elbowed Belsnickle aside.

But he did not become fixed on Christmas (rather than either his feast day or New Year's) until the 1823 publication of Clement Moore's "A Visit from Saint Nicholas." Moore moved the saint definitively to Christmas Eve. Although inspired by Irving, Moore swapped out Santa's wagon for a sleigh and multiplied the reindeer, who had already begun to replace the horse. From now on there would be eight of them, complete with names—though few of those who can recite all the names realize that Donder and Blitzen are just German for Thunder and Lightning. Rudolph, the ninth reindeer, originally dreamed up as a marketing gimmick for the Montgomery Ward department store, was added to Santa's sleigh-team only after World War II.

Clement Moore's Santa was a jolly elf, with none of a bishop's dignity or authority, and his reindeer were tiny. Other depictions of Santa at the time sometimes had him wearing a Revolutionary-era three-cornered hat, a short

Dutch blue jacket, red knee-length trousers (called knick-erbockers and associated with the Dutch), yellow stockings, and ice skates. The modern visual version of Santa, a plus-sized man with a bushy white beard, wearing a red fur-trimmed coat (red of course being the color of a bishop's formal vestments), only became standard in the 1860s with the cartoons of Thomas Nast.

Nast, a New York political commentator and cartoonist, now known principally for his long battle against corruption in the city's government ("Tammany Hall"), depicted a Santa Claus with all the attributes he had been accumulating for half a century, plus, in addition, a toy workshop. Although he has continued to develop, a century and a half later his Santa is immediately recognizable: white-bearded, jolly and plump (though, for Nast, still small enough to fit down a chimney), crowned with holly and dressed in furs. The long Dutch pipe that his Santa smoked has, however, been quietly edited out.

The visual depiction of Santa took essentially its final form in Coca-Cola commercials from the 1930s. In these ads, which unabashedly appealed to children, Thomas Nast's Santa underwent his final reworking in illustrations by Haddon Sundblom.

Santa in these commercials is now enormously fat, making his ability to slide down a chimney as much a marvel as his ability to visit all the world's children in a single night. The European bringers of Christmas presents can be quite gaunt, but not the American Santa. His rosy-cheeked face has a resolutely cheerful expression, conveying friendly engagement with other Coke drinkers. He wears bright red—Coca-Cola red—velvet jacket and trousers, trimmed with white fur, now standard. He has the broad black belt and tall black boots that any modern Santa costume requires. By now images of the reindeer have been replaced almost universally by American white-tailed deer (still, however, called reindeer).

Sipping a Coke rather than smoking his pipe, this

commercial version of Santa embodies all of Christmas's contradictions: encouraging people to buy (in this case buy a soft drink) while suggesting that a real Christmas is based on boundless joy and generosity, coming not from the store and obtained not with money, but from somewhere distant and magical and unconnected to commerce.

6. SANTA CLAUS IN THE MODERN ERA

Magical beings from afar can come to punish as well as to reward. In their own way, modern stories of Santa recapitulate stories of Judgment Day. A day is coming when all shall be judged: the good rewarded, the wicked punished. The original, early nineteenth-century Santa brought simple presents, like a doll or a top, to good children, but a switch for bad children, to make it easier for their parents to beat them.

In modern America, pretty much everybody who believes in Heaven assumes they will go there. Few worry that they'll be sent to Hell. In the same way, all children are assumed to be good. "He knows if you've been sleeping, he knows when you're awake, he knows if you've been bad or good, so be good for goodness' sake." The song still warns of punishment, while presenting Santa as a form of NSA-surveillance, but in practice American children do not have to worry that Santa will spurn them.

Part of the true meaning that Santa provides to Christmas is that it is, one gathers, good to lie to small children—and not just about the surveillance. American parents routinely insist that Santa, not they, provided the presents under the tree and encourage children to leave out milk and cookies for Saint Nick, even carrots for his reindeer. Aunts and uncles are cautioned not to say anything that would challenge the simple faith of tots who "still believe in Santa Claus." I myself, the oldest child in our family, was still writing letters to Santa at the age of ten (he always failed to come through, however).

It would seem to undercut the very idea of Christmas as joyous and religiously-based to discover that a major part of its celebration is based on deception. Yet, surprisingly, very few children act betrayed when they realize that all the guys in the red suits who have been labeled "Santa's helpers" actually have no one to whom to report. Stories and reality are not rigidly separated when one is small, and learning something that the littler children do not yet know may give some youngsters a source of secret pride.

At some point children work out that adults lie all the time, and it doesn't bother them if they sense it's being done with good intentions and for their benefit. "The power is out and the thermometer is dropping—it will be so much fun to spend the night sleeping by the fireplace!"

Parental lies about Santa's existence seem designed to make Christmas magical, other-worldly, something beyond the normal physical rules of the universe. The toys he brings were made by elves, not by factory workers in China. It may well be that it is the parents, not the children themselves, who desperately want to believe in Santa, who want to enter into a myth where generosity is not commercialized, where gifts are hand crafted (by elves), and where Christmas connects our mundane world with a world of universal love.

The famous editorial, "Yes, Virginia, there is a Santa Claus," originally published in 1897 and reprinted in many papers on Christmas Eve even now, defines Santa as "love and generosity and devotion." This was essentially how my own parents broke Santa's non-existence to me when I was ten. As a personification of a spirit of giving and of special experiences far beyond the ordinary, Santa has to be considered part of the true meaning of Christmas.

But one still wonders if the reduction of Santa to happy metaphor ever transfers over to stories about the Christ child, who, theologically, is supposed to have been entirely real.

7. CHRISTMAS IN THE MIDDLE AGES

The Middle Ages had no trouble celebrating Christmas as a religious holiday. Doubts whether December 25 really was Jesus's birthday never surfaced. Indeed, churchmen argued that as Christmas is December 25, then Mary must have become pregnant on March 25, and that therefore, obviously, the Crucifixion occurred on March 25, because people (or at least important people) tend to die on the same day as their conception, "as we all know."

Christmas Day was celebrated with Masses, with singing, and with great feasts. The songs were all theologically informed (no "Frosty the Snowman" here), with a special emphasis on the doctrine that, as from Adam all shall die, so with Christ shall all be made alive. Christmas Day thus marked the coming of salvation to sinful humans, who had all, according to medieval Christianity, gone straight to Hell from the time of Adam and Eve right down to the Crucifixion.

There were no Christmas trees, no Santa equivalents, and no Christmas presents, though there was probably a fair amount of drinking. Medieval people did celebrate the entire Twelve Days of Christmas, so December 25 was just the beginning of the celebration, not the end, as it can be in the US. (I once knew a woman, tidy to a fault, who said that her favorite day of the year was December 26, "Because then I can take down the tree and throw out the mess.")

New Year's Day was the day for presents in the Middle Ages, but there was no sense that presents were especially for children. Rather, gift-giving included tokens distributed by great lords to those who served them and special presents exchanged between lovers. Gifts at New Year's were a tradition that went back to pagan Rome, as preachers intermittently warned people, urging them to give up such a non-Christian practice, but such preaching had little if any effect.

Children's special holiday was not Christmas Day but rather December 28, the Feast of the Innocents. This feast day celebrated those who were considered the very first Christian martyrs: the children whom Herod slaughtered in his unsuccessful effort to find and kill the baby who was prophesied to be greater than he. (Stephen, put to death in the Book of Acts, was also considered the first Christian martyr. Martyrdom is important enough that it can support a number of different "firsts.")

December 28 was sometimes called the Feast of Fools, because it honored not only children but anyone of limited understanding. It was backwards day, a day for inversions, when things were allowed or even encouraged that would not be allowed the rest of the year. For example, there might be the equivalent of a Christmas pageant, celebrating Mary and Joseph fleeing into Egypt to escape Herod's killers, in which a live donkey would be brought into church.

Although in modern America religion is usually assumed to make people quiet and obedient, medieval people knew that Christianity is fundamentally subversive. It challenges received assumptions while denying that the rich and powerful are better than the poor—in fact, it asserts the opposite. The last shall be first. The meek shall inherit the earth. A celebration based on inversion, right in the middle of the Twelve Days of Christmas, was thus considered inherently Christian.

At some medieval monasteries, one of the boys being trained as a future monk would play the role of the abbot for the day, giving nonsensical commands, and there was always a great deal of shouting and running around. Besides celebrating inversion and being an opportunity to let off steam, such a holiday of course ultimately reinforced the normal structures: it was obviously ridiculous that a boy should be in the position to express an opinion or to give orders.

Interestingly, in spite of such apparent contradictions, medieval people did not worry about the true meaning of Christmas. It seemed self-evident: Christ was born to bring salvation.

At the end of the Middle Ages, however, there began to be a nostalgia for an "old-fashioned" Christmas. This nostalgia permeates the Arthurian story, "Sir Gawain and the Green Knight." Written in the late fourteenth or fifteenth century and set in a mythical and distant past, the story suggests that in the good old days of King Arthur people celebrated the Christmas season with church services, presents, feasting, flirting, dancing, hunting, playful games and tournaments, and unanticipated marvels.

The chief marvel of the story is the Green Knight, who goads Sir Gawain into cutting his head off, which activity he calls a "Christmas pastime." He then rides away with his head under his arm, reminding Gawain that *he* will have his head cut off in compensation next Christmas.

The story goes on to involve a Green Chapel that looks remarkably like an ancient pagan tumulus and Gawain's efforts to resist being seduced by a lord's wife, while worrying about his soul and his upcoming decapitation, as well as themes of honor and humiliation. It's a great Christmas story. But what happens to Gawain? you ask. I don't want to give away the ending. Read it for yourself!

One of the most striking aspects of the story is that the modern world is not the first to find that Christmas has somehow become too modern, whatever that may mean.

8. AN OLD-FASHIONED CHRISTMAS

Six centuries after the composition of "Sir Gawain" and the end of the Middle Ages, we still want to make our Christmases more like the Christmases of olden days. An "old-fashioned" Christmas is now universally agreed to be much closer to Christmas's true meaning than a resolutely new-fangled celebration. But how far back do we want to go in finding that old-fashioned celebration?

Probably not to medieval monks allowing a donkey into church and arguing that the first Good Friday fell on the anniversary of the Annunciation. And of course we do not wish to have the "old fashioned" version of wassail, where bands of lower-class people quite literally invaded the houses of their landlords, demanding—and getting— beer and good food.

No one wants to return to the raucous carousing that celebrated the Christmas holiday in the sixteenth through seventeenth centuries—and which has now found a new home on New Year's Eve—or the Puritan reaction of forbidding the celebration of Christmas altogether. Nor do we wish to return to the olden days of the eighteenth century, when Christmas, while not forbidden, was barely celebrated at all.

"Old-fashioned" when it comes to Christmas essentially equates in the modern US with the nineteenth century. And yet those who lived in the old-fashioned times we would like to imitate asserted that they wished they could return to how Christmas was celebrated in an even earlier time. Washington Irving, who essentially created the nostalgic ideal of "Old Christmas," was after all writing two centuries ago.

The specifics of Irving's "holiday customs and rural games" have however tended to fade (who in the US—or even Britain—wants to celebrate the holiday with Morris dancing?), leaving only the general sense that Christmas was better in days of yore. We instead yearn for the Christmas of Charles Dickens, even though modern readers tend to sentimentalize his "A Christmas Carol," originally published in 1843 and probably the most influential book ever on "the true meaning of Christmas." Dickens himself was a fierce advocate for the poor, who he thought were being blamed for their own misfortunes, and whom he believed the well-to-do were morally obligated to help. This message is now downplayed, in favor of the book's heavy dose of nostalgia.

Rather ironically, Dickens himself was nostalgic for a bygone time, a supposedly simpler and certainly old-fashioned era that had already passed when he was writing. "A Christmas Carol" harks back to era he believed already gone, an era of good cheer and family celebration.

But this beloved classic does not match the modern version of what Christmas is supposed to be like. There is notably no religious celebration in "A Christmas Carol." Christmas in the story is celebrated as a series of family parties and dances, focused on a blazing pudding, preferably with a large fowl to eat first. There is no Santa Claus, and few if any gifts. Stores are open in spite of the holiday. It is a management concession that employees are allowed to have the day off. (This was not a uniquely English feature. American factories were also running on December 25 in the mid- nineteenth century.) Scrooge learns the true meaning of Christmas from a collection of rather un-Christian "spirits." And there may be holly and mistletoe, but there are no Christmas trees.

Christmas trees appear to have begun in Germany, by at least the late eighteenth century. It is perhaps ironic that this ultimate symbol of an old-fashioned Christmas should have begun in German lands, which had not even been thoroughly Christianized until seven or eight centuries after Christianity's beginnings.

This German tradition seems to have first reached New England in the 1830s, among the well-to-do who had heard or read about them and thought they could provide something special for the children. Parents had been trying, ever since industrially-manufactured toys became widely available, to make each Christmas more special than the one before, and a tree lit with candles, on whose branches toys and candy dangled, certainly made a spectacular sight. The novelty of bringing a pine tree indoors was especially appealing because it could be described as "old fashioned."

Queen Victoria of England, whose husband, Prince Albert, was German, established the cult of Christmas trees in England in the 1840s. As well as setting the (then) record for length of a British monarch's reign and presiding over the British Empire, Victoria popularized the white wedding dress and Mendelssohn's Bridal March even before doing the same for the Christmas tree.

From then on, well-to-do Brits felt compelled to bring large evergreens into the house to celebrate, a custom that spread quickly to the rest of society and to other parts of Europe and the world. The nineteenth-century ritual of erecting a Christmas tree was intended to make Christmas more traditional and less commercial, indicating that even in the supposedly "old fashioned" nineteenth century there was a concerted search for old-fashioned values. The emphasis on the tree was intended then to move the chief focus of the Christmas celebration into the home, out of the streets and taverns—so that modern shopping malls, with trees galore, have to imply that shopping in a public place is somehow being "home."

Roughly half of all American households now put up a tree. These trees are so important that evergreens are cut, baled, and sent overseas to troops serving in places like Afghanistan, because it would be (apparently) impossible to celebrate Christmas without a tree, especially in an arid Muslim country.

But if one thinks about it, bringing an evergreen indoors in the dead of winter has distinctly pagan overtones: the tree represents the continuity of life and the rebirth of the sun's return after the solstice. Yet a good old-fashioned Christmas requires a tree, a real one, not an artificial one. An authentic-looking artificial one may just possibly pass (even if missing pine scent), but a white tufted object in the vague shape of a tree cannot be considered to represent "the true meaning of Christmas," even if the machine bathing it in a sequence of glowing colors is also tinkling out "Silent Night."

The family in a TV show who thinks it acceptable to have a white tufted object will learn within the hour that a real pine tree is preferable, even if (or especially if) it is somewhat short and misshapen.

Dragging a dead tree to the curb a week or two after Christmas, where it sheds the rest of its needles while awaiting the inglorious fate of being tossed into the landfill with broken toys and coffee grounds, in no way diminishes its centrality to a meaningful Christmas.

Germany has its own version of an old-fashioned Christmas, the *Christkindlmarkt,* or Christ-child market. In the weeks leading up to Christmas, thousands of towns large and small sell crafts and food from little pine-trimmed booths in the town square in the evenings, under strings of glittering lights. The ornaments and beeswax candles are made by local artisans, and bratwurst and gingerbread keep hunger at bay. Caroling or ice skating can add to the fun. The tradition goes back centuries, and the largest, Stuttgart's, claims 4 million visitors a year. Many of those who attend have done so essentially every year of their lives. All visitors, both Germans and tourists, agree that the *Christkindlmarkt* represents an old-fashioned, authentic Christmas celebration.

Strikingly, this old-fashioned Christmas is so appealing that it has begun to be imported into other countries, including France and the US. Here a brand new tradition is created, claiming not to be new at all. Feeling deeply nostalgic for a past that never existed for them, parents eager to show their children the true meaning of Christmas start taking them to the *Christkindlmarkt* so that they can revel in its traditions.

9. CHRISTMAS AROUND THE WORLD

Part of the difficulty of determining Christmas's true meaning is that there are so many varied traditions competing for dominance. Different European countries and different American regions all assert that they are following the old-fashioned ways of their particular area. They may share a great deal in common, but Christmas brings out the local.

Even what might be considered the basic or standard American Christmas celebration already has elements from several continents and several millennia, none of which completely match. We have Christmas trees and Advent calendars from Germany, Christmas stockings from the Dutch (replacing shoes), Christmas cards from the British, and roast turkey from the Americas. We have remnants of pagan solstice revels, including Saturnalia from the ancient Romans and the Yule log and mistletoe from ancient northern Europeans. (Though I must say it remains mysterious how mistletoe, the plant that tragically killed the beloved Norse god Balduir, has come to require holiday kisses.)

And then not only every region but every family in every region develops its own traditions, such as Great-aunt

Agatha's chestnut dressing, or the requirement that each child wait quietly until the next child has unwrapped a gift, or new pajamas for Christmas Eve, or photos on Christmas Day around the tree, or going to see the *Nutcracker* the week before Christmas, or ....

Just as an American bride, planning a wedding rivaling a luxury car in price, may borrow the horse-drawn carriage from one wedding she saw or read about, the string quartet from another, and the chocolate fountain from a third, so anyone planning "the best Christmas ever" may seize upon any elements that seems meaningful from any tradition and incorporate them.

This is complicated by children's assumptions that the Christmas traditions that have "always" been observed in their families (for at least a half dozen years!) are the only correct ones. Celebrating with cousins who expect pecan waffles on Christmas morning even before taking down the stockings, or whose Christmas tree is decorated with the wrong kind of lights (flashing or non-flashing, white or colored), or who are allowed to open a select present as early as December 23, is not just mistaken but outright heretical.

This is further complicated by the rest of the world's embrace of American Christmas. The Japanese in particular love Christmas. Without the slightest concern about the birth of Christ, they celebrate the day with gifts and decorations and sing Japanese songs to the tune of American songs (such as "Jingle Bells"), where, to the English-speaker, "Santa" may be the only recognizable word). The imagery in Japanese ads urging people to buy presents and dine at expensive restaurants suggests that Christmas is especially a time not for families but rather for young, loving couples.

Other nominally Christian communities in different parts of the world have their own, distinctive traditions. In New Zealand, Christmas is often celebrated with a barbecue. In Trinidad, Christmas is the time to repaint the house and reupholster the furniture. Among the Inuit (Eskimos) on the North Slope of Alaska, Christmas is marked by community festivals, drumming, dancing, and games. During Advent in Sweden, girls celebrate Saint Lucia's Day (December 13) by wearing a wreath of candles on their heads and bringing the coffee. Italian children look forward to a visit from Befana, the bad fairy who refused to accompany the Wise Men to Bethlehem, regretted her decision, and has been making gifts to children ever since in the hopes of finding the right one. The English eat their big family Christmas dinner early so that they will be through in time to hear the queen give her mid-afternoon radio broadcast.

Once one takes Christmas apart into its elements, it becomes obvious that there never was a "true" form of Christmas celebration in some vaguely-defined old-fashioned time. Rather, we have invented Christmas's traditions, asserting those traditions as old and hallowed by many generations' use, even when they are not.

But this is not the point. Once we realize that everyone celebrates Christmas at least somewhat differently, we should be free to choose whichever traditions we want to incorporate. It does not matter whether a tradition is ancient or modern, something with centuries-long roots or something brand new. If it is meaningful to us, then it is by definition meaningful. After all, we are the ones inventing tradition, so we can invent any tradition we like.

10. CHRISTMAS AS NOSTALGIA

If people have yearned for an old-fashioned, traditional Christmas for centuries, each generation finding the current one deficient in comparison to earlier ones, does this mean that Christmas has been going steadily downhill? Does the previous generation's or century's version of Christmas somehow seem better only because it is one step less degraded?

Fortunately, there is a better explanation.

The nostalgia of Christmas is compounded of memories of one's own upbringing. Someone whose family always had a Christmas turkey will continue to require one for an old-fashioned Christmas and reject a ham without a second thought—and vice versa. The continued prevalence of fruitcake, which few will admit actually liking, can only be explained by nostalgia. Just as we had to sit on Santa's lap and eat fruitcake, so must the next generation.

Every family has its own traditions, some of which continue practices going back generations, some of which were deliberate choices, some of which were almost accidental in origin. It doesn't matter. What matters is repeating those traditions.

An old-fashioned Christmas requires that, if possible,

everyone be "home," however home is defined, in order to reenact the traditions of one's youth in the most authentic setting. For young adults it means returning to their parents' home to take the old, familiar ornaments out of the box, retelling the story of the time that everyone went sledding on Christmas and Cousin Frank broke his collar bone, and eating turkey with the chestnut dressing that Great-aunt Agatha made once forty years ago, and which has carried on without her ever since.

The hassle of traveling home during the holidays does undercut, however, one of the mandates of an old-fashioned Christmas, which is that it should be joyful and free of stress. And adult siblings are always irritated to discover that the brother or sister with whom they are delighted to be sharing Christmas again is just as big a pain now as they were when growing up.

Parents of small children, who can plausibly argue that the grandparents should come to them rather than vice versa, may be able to avoid travel problems but they too feel stressed. So when and how did this stress-free old-fashioned Christmas actually operate?

The answer surely is that the Christmas we remember nostalgically is the Christmas of childhood, when our parents may have been rushed and worried, but we never noticed. When the month between Thanksgiving and Christmas feels as long as the rest of the year put together, there can be no sense of desperate urgency. When frantically cleaning the guest room for Grandma and meeting her at the airport is someone else's concern, the only issues are how many presents she has crammed into her luggage and whether she'll be baking cookies again.

Children see their friends at school daily, so there is no need to plan and prepare for getting together with them. Token presents for Mom and Dad or siblings do not require reworking the entire household budget. (When I was little, a common present that we siblings exchanged was a package of chewing gum. Individual sticks could be taken out of the wrapper and individually wrapped for different recipients.) Because children believe they want only the presents that any sensible child would want, there is by definition no artificially created hankering after material goods. The old-fashioned Christmas for which we yearn is a Christmas of happy ignorance, when gift-buying and cleaning and decorating and cooking were carried out by others.

Those parents standing in line at the mall, desperately trying to make the checkbook balance, should be assured that their children will look back at this time as one when people still knew how to have an old-fashioned Christmas.

11. THE TRUE MEANING OF CHRISTMAS

So what in fact is the true meaning of Christmas? Does it even have one? Why do we feel compelled to keep searching for it?

Most of those who celebrate Christmas would agree that a "true" Christmas is compounded of beautifully decorated homes smelling delightfully of pine and baked goods; good cheer with family and close friends; quiet religious observance; special foods not seen for much of the year; glittering lights that make an evening snowy street appear almost magical; joyous music; and well thought-out gifts to bring surprise and delight to children and even adults.

This is to be obtained, of course, without overspending, without losing one's temper or one's car keys while pushing through a crowded mall, without the children whining for some foolish toy, without attending parties where drinking takes precedence over fellowship, without cutting or burning oneself in the kitchen while grimly cooking up a festive feast, and without falling off the stepladder while hanging the decorations.

It is quite touching that, every year, we decide that this is possible.

The reason that there is, every year, so much debate about the "true" meaning of Christmas is because so many expectations are piled onto one holiday, many of them non-congruent if not indeed contradictory.

In 1915, on Christmas Eve, Thomas Hardy published a short poem, "The Oxen," in which an old man, back in the nineteenth century, told the young folks that the oxen all kneel down at midnight on Christmas Eve, and none of them doubted it. By 1915, when England was engrossed in World War I, such thoughts could seem silly—"So fair a fancy few would weave/ In these years!" Hardy says in the poem. But then he adds, if someone invited him now to return to the cow barn of his childhood to see the oxen kneeling, "I should go with him in the gloom/ Hoping it might be so."

Hoping it might be so. Wishing to believe. There is Christmas's true meaning.

Parents tell children Santa comes to bring them toys. The hymns tell us that Christ comes to save sinners. Both the parents and the hymns seem very sure about it. At Christmas even the cynical can come close to believing.

This year, surely, we can have mounds of presents without commercialization, family get-togethers without sibling squabbles, feasts without worrying about food allergies or gaining weight, Christmas specials to watch on TV without replacing family interactions with electronic media, a month or more packed full of celebration and holiday events without becoming stressed or financially stretched or just plain exhausted. This year, we will be better people.

At Christmas we all want to become the parents, aunts and uncles, or grandparents we either wished we had or imagined we had, the wise, unflustered ones who cooked up delicious meals from scratch, who loved to surprise us, who could transform a mundane living room into a place of magic, who knew how to make good things happen. At Christmas we want the whole family together, at home, not scattered from office to fast-food eatery to soccer game to the mall. At Christmas, we all want to believe that a baby born two thousand years ago can somehow bring about peace on earth.

Maybe it really could be so. Every baby cannot be the Christ child. But every child does come into the world with enormous potential, having done no wrong yet in spite of whatever trouble the parents may be in, ready to learn to smile and laugh as well as to eat and cry and sleep. Children may not require gold, frankincense, and myrrh, but they do require love and care. If we are wise, wise men or wise women, we should heed.

FURTHER READING

Archer, Sarah. *Midcentury Christmas: Holiday Fads, Fancy, and Fun from 1945 to 1970*. New York, 2016.

Bouchard, Constance B. "Dreaming of an 'Old-Fashioned' Yule." *Los Angeles Times*, November 29, 1985. http://articles.latimes.com/1985-11-29/news/vw-5017_1_old-fashioned-christmas

Bowler, Gerry. *The World Encyclopedia of Christmas*. Toronto, 2000.

______. *Santa Claus: A Biography*. Toronto, 2005.

Dickens, Charles. "A Christmas Carol." In *Christmas Books*. The Oxford Illustrated Dickens. Oxford, 1954 [originally published in 1843].

Hardy, Thomas. "The Oxen" [poem with accompanying commentary on this official website, originally published in 1915]. www.hardysociety.org/files/ download/244

Harris, Max. *Sacred Folly: A New History of the Feast of Fools*. Ithaca, NY, 2011.

Irving, Washington. *Knickerbocker's History of New York*. 2 vols. New York, 1894 [originally published in 1809].

______. *The Sketch-Book*. New York, 1864 [originally published in 1819].

Jones, Charles W. *Saint Nicholas of Myra, Bari, and Manhattan: Biography of a Legend*. Chicago, 1978.

Llana, Susan Miller. "The German Roots of Christmas." *The Christian Science Monitor,* December 23, 2013, pp. 21–23.

Miller, Daniel, ed. *Unwrapping Christmas*. Oxford, 1993.

Moore, Clement Clarke. "A Visit from St. Nicholas" [originally published in 1823]. http://www.poetryfoundation. org/poem/171924

Nissenbaum, Stephen. *The Battle for Christmas*. New York, 1996.

Pendergrast, Mark. *For God, Country and Coca-Cola: The Definitive History of the Great American Soft Drink and the Company that Makes It*. 2nd ed. New York, 2000.

Seal, Jeremy. *Nicholas: The Epic Journey from Saint to Santa Claus*. New York, 2005.

Seuss, Dr. *How the Grinch Stole Christmas*. New York, 1957.

"Sir Gawain and the Green Knight." In J.R.R. Tolkien, trans. *Sir Gawain and the Green Knight, Pearl, Sir Orfeo*. London, 1975.

"Yes, Virginia, There is a Santa Claus" [originally published in 1897]. http://www.newseum.org/yesvirginia/

ABOUT THE AUTHOR

C. Dale Brittain is both a fantasy writer and a professor of medieval history, having been writing stories since she was five years old. Her early love of knights and castles was cemented by a trip to Europe with her family during high school. She blogs at cdalebrittain.blogspot.com, covering both medieval social history and her fantasy novels.

www.ingramcontent.com/pod-product-compliance
Lightning Source LLC
Chambersburg PA
CBHW061738250726
48657CB00002B/998